D0783688

Other books in this series:
Flowers a Celebration   Cats a Celebration
Teddy Bears a Celebration   Golf a Celebration
Roses a Celebration   Birds a Celebration

Published simultaneously in 1993 by Exley Publications
in Great Britain, and Exley Giftbooks in the USA.

Selection and arrangement ©Helen Exley 1993.
ISBN 1-85015-444-9

Edited by Helen Exley.
Designed by Pinpoint Design.
Typeset by Delta, Watford.
Text researched by Margaret Montgomery.
Printed and bound by William Clowes, Beccles, UK.

Exley Publications Ltd, 16 Chalk Hill, Watford, Herts WD1 4BN, U.K.
Exley Giftbooks, 359 East Main Street, Suite 3D, Mount Kisco,
NY 10549, USA.

Picture Credits: Bridgeman Art Library: Cover, title page, pages 6, 33, 34, 41,
43, 45, 49, 50, 56, 59, 61. Bury Art Gallery: page 45. Fine Art Photographic
Library Ltd: pages 8, 11, 17, 18, 20, 24, 27, 29, 31, 37, 39, 47, 54. Roy Miles
Gallery: page 50. Scala: pages 14 and 52. Image Select: page 13.

CHRISTMAS

A CELEBRATION
IN WORDS
AND PAINTINGS

SELECTED BY
HELEN EXLEY

EXLEY
MT. KISCO, NEW YORK • WATFORD, UK

Christmas is hugs and "Oh - you *shouldn't* have! It's *great!*" Christmas is feuds cancelled, friendships renewed. Christmas is a break from reality.

CLARA ORTEGA

❄

Welcome, everything! Welcome, alike what has been, and what never was, and what we hope may be, to your shelter underneath the holly, to your places round the Christmas fire, where what is sits open-hearted!

CHARLES DICKENS (1812-1870)
FROM *"WHAT CHRISTMAS IS AS WE GROW OLDER"*, 1851

❄

The angel did not call blessings down on all good people - but on people of goodwill. Ordinary people, fallible people, people simply doing the best they can.

And so let's join in wishing all those people - our friends, our relatives in this small planet - known and unknown, of every country, every creed - a very, very Happy Christmas.

PAM BROWN, b.1928

LOVE AT CHRISTMAS TIME

It's your love your friends need - never expensive gifts or extravagant surprises.

MARION GARRETTY, b.1917

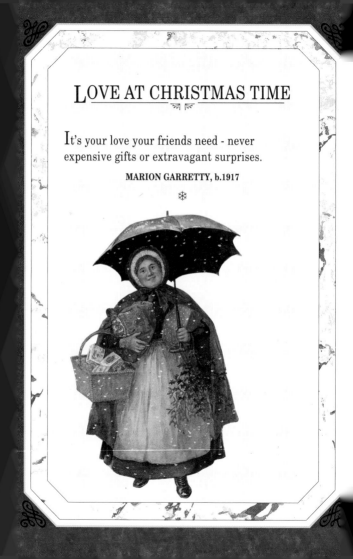

Christmas is a time of Do You Remember?
Of family jokes.
Of family rituals.
Sometimes a little sadness
- but always love.

PAM BROWN, b.1928

❄

To open the door and find the one you thought
couldn't possibly make it standing there - *that's*
the best of Christmas presents.

HELEN THOMSON, b.1943

❄

Christmas means...children, family, cards and
mince pies; kissing under mistletoe, music and
myrrh, puddings and jelly beans, candy and
toys, almonds, angels and gingerbread cookies,
lumpy Christmas stockings and three wise men;
dolls, drums, ham and holly, Santa Claus,
walnuts,... carols and candles, jingle bells,
fruitcake, gold, garlands and gifts...but most of
all Christmas means love.

MARIAN FRENCH
FROM *"THE JOYS OF CHRISTMAS"*

HOME FOR CHRISTMAS

This is meeting time again. Home is the magnet. The winter land roars and hums with the eager speed of return journeys. The dark is noisy and bright with late-night arrivals - doors thrown open, running shadows on snow, open arms, kisses, voices and laughter, laughter at everything and nothing. Inarticulate, giddying and confused are those original minutes of being back again. The very familiarity of everything acts like shock. Contentment has to be drawn in slowly, steadyingly, in deep breaths, there is so much of it. We rely on home not to change, and it does not, wherefore we give thanks. Again Christmas: abiding point of return. Set apart by its mystery, mood and magic, the season seems in a way to stand outside time. All that is dear, that is lasting, renews its hold on us: we are home again....

ELIZABETH BOWEN (1899-1973)
FROM *"HOME FOR CHRISTMAS"*

❄

And I *do* come home at Christmas. We all do, or we all should. We all come home, or ought to come home, for a short holiday - the longer, the better ... to take, and give a rest.

CHARLES DICKENS (1812-1870)

❄

What will go into the Christmas Stocking
While the clock on the mantelpiece goes
tick-tocking?
    An orange, a penny,
    Some sweets, not too many,
    A trumpet, a dolly,
    A sprig of green holly,
    A book and a top,
    And a grocery shop,
    Some beads in a box,
    An ass and an ox,
    And a lamb, plain and good,
    All whittled in wood,
    A white sugar dove,
    A handful of love,
    Another of fun,
    And it's very near done -
    A big silver star
    On top - there you are!
Come morning you'll wake to the clock's
tick-tocking,
And that's what you'll find in the Christmas
Stocking.

ELEANOR FARJEON (1881-1965)

❄

Last year I heard Santa Claus knocking on the door.

Daddy let him in and I saw him in my bedroom with his red coat on.

I kept my eyes shut.

DAVID SKIDMORE, AGE 5

❄

Small daughter: "How many more days is it before Christmas?"
Mother: "Not many. Why do you ask?"
Small daughter: "I just wondered if it's near enough for me to start being a good little girl."

❊

Somehow you know that giving should be more fun than receiving but it isn't.

CHARLOTTE BEATTIE, AGE 10

❊

Dear Santa Claus,
Please can I have just one teddy bear this Christmas, nothing else but a teddy bear.
From Sophia.
P.S. Please can teddy have a portable TV to keep teddy amused when I'm at school?

SOPHIA JONES, AGE 9

❊

Christmas is the only day when children get up early without being told to.

SIMON MORGAN, AGE 10

❊

FATHER CHRISTMAS

On Christmas Eve all over the world children hang their stockings and eagerly await the arrival of Santa Claus....

Endowed with extraordinary powers, he is without human limitations, is able to circumnavigate the globe in one single night and has no difficulty in being in countless places at one time.

Known as Father Christmas to the English, Père Noël to the French, Sinterclaus to the Dutch. The Germans call him Christkindl. The Chinese have their Lam Khoong Khoong, meaning Nice Old Father, and the Japanese have Hoteisho, who has eyes in both the back and front of his head and carries a big bag of toys. On Epiphany Eve in Italy the good little witch Befana comes down the chimney on a broom and fills the shoes of good Italian boys and girls with toys.

MARIAN FRENCH
FROM *"THE JOYS OF CHRISTMAS"*

❄

I can remember as a small child the almost unbearable feeling of joy when the same old cardboard box was brought down from the attic and familiar decorations were taken out of their tissue paper. No matter that many were faded or broken, it was important that they were the same as last year and the year before. Then there was the sweet anticipation of opening the advent calendar. Later there were particularly special evenings when, as the eldest of four, I would stay up after my brothers and sister had gone to bed and help my mother to make the mince pies and ice the cake.

We all brought home cards, calendars and presents made at school and Sunday School. Carols were rehearsed for the carol service on squeaky recorders, and Mother's old evening dresses were adapted for the nativity play and pantomime. For the whole of December the kitchen seemed to smell of cinnamon, cloves and baking. Cards arrived and arrangements were made for family visits. It was a long delicious party, and I wanted it to last forever.

FRANCINE LAWRENCE

There are people who will tell you that Christmas is not what it used to be. . . . Never heed such dismal reminiscences. There are few men who have lived long enough in the world, who cannot call up such thoughts any day in the year. Then do not select the merriest of the three hundred and sixty-five, for your doleful recollections, but draw your chair nearer the blazing fire - fill the glass and send round the song . . . and thank God it's no worse. . . . Reflect upon your present blessings - of which every man has many - not on your past misfortunes, of which all men have some. Fill your glass again, with a merry face and contented heart. Our life on it, but your Christmas shall be merry, and your new year a happy one!

CHARLES DICKENS (1812-1870)

❄

The only real blind person at Christmastime is he who has not Christmas in his heart.

HELEN KELLER (1880-1968)
FROM *"THE LADIES HOME JOURNAL"*, 1906

❄

NATIVITY

Every Christmas, thousands of tiny Marys are attended by shepherds in teatowels and angels with tinsel haloes, and at each children's Nativity play, with stifled giggles and stuttered words, the mystery of the Christmas story reveals itself again. Mothers stay up late sewing costumes and adults frantically try to coordinate the whole event, rehearsing reluctant or over-excited children and expecting a theatrical disaster.

But it never is a disaster. Instead, something almost mystical happens - a kind of solemnity tinged with joy which comes over everyone involved, from the tiniest woolly sheep or sheeted angel to the proudest grandparent in the audience. Every Nativity play is a triumph in its own way with meaning for all those involved.

FRANCINE LAWRENCE
FROM *"COUNTRY LIVING, COUNTRY CHRISTMAS"*

❄

We are a most blundering, stupid, greedy, selfish and unbalanced species. And yet - believers and non-believers alike, we gaze at the newborn child in the manger and hope, every year, that out of such innocence can grow the wisdom and the love we lack.

PAM BROWN, b.1928

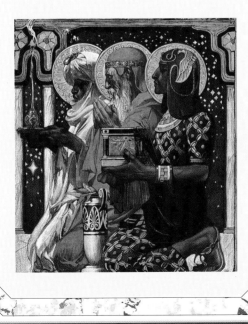

At Christmas there are small, splendid
pleasures.
Stealing raisins when Mother makes the
pudding.
Licking out the mixing bowl. Hiding things.
Getting out the Best Glasses.
Eating chocolate ginger straight after breakfast.
Walking off the meal. Snoozing.

PAM BROWN, b.1928

One of the greatest delights of Christmas, especially for children, is to bring down from the attic or from the back of a cupboard the box containing decorations and special things kept for Christmas each year. The things that were carefully packed away last year come out looking magically different. Fresh and unexpected, they seem to hold in them all the excitement and anticipation that will infect the household right up to the day itself. They are like old friends that one is pleased to see.

FRANCINE LAWRENCE
FROM *"COUNTRY LIVING, COUNTRY CHRISTMAS"*

❄

Time was with most of us, when Christmas Day, encircling all our limited world like a magic ring, left nothing out for us to miss or seek; bound together all our home enjoyments, affections, and hopes, grouped everything and everyone round the Christmas fire, and made the little picture shining in our bright young eyes complete.

CHARLES DICKENS (1812-1870)

❄

Christmas was close at hand, in all his bluff and hearty honesty; it was the season of hospitality, merriment, and open-heartedness; the old year was preparing, like an ancient philosopher, to call his friends around him, and amidst the sound of feasting and revelry to pass gently and calmly away. Gay and merry was the time, and gay and merry were at least four of the numerous hearts that were gladdened by its coming.

And numerous indeed are the hearts to which Christmas brings a brief season of happiness and enjoyment.

How many families, whose members have been dispersed and scattered far and wide, in the restless struggles of life, are then reunited, and meet once again in that happy state of companionship and mutual good-will, which is a source of such pure and unalloyed delight, and one so incompatible with the cares and sorrows of the world, that the religious belief of the most civilized nations, and the rude traditions of the roughest savages, alike number it among the first joys of a future condition of existence, provided for the blest and happy! How many old recollections, and how many dormant sympathies, does Christmas time awaken!

CHARLES DICKENS (1812-1870)
FROM *"THE PICKWICK PAPERS"*

❄

REMEMBER THEM

The shops close. Families turn inward. The streets are full of people going somewhere they're expected. Now is the time when the lonely feel their isolation. This is the time the poor recognize their poverty.

If only everyone could feel wanted this Christmas!

MAYA V. PATEL, b. 1943

❄

Before you bid, for Christmas' sake,
   Your guests to sit at meat,
Oh please to save a little cake
   For them that have no treat....

Before you gather round the tree
   To dance the day about,
Oh please to give a little glee
   To them that go without.

ELEANOR FARJEON (1881-1965)
EXTRACT FROM *"FOR THEM"*

❄

On Christmas Eve I hung at the foot of my bed Bessie Bunter's black stocking, and always, I said, I would stay awake all the moonlit, snowlit night to hear the roof-alighting reindeer and see the hollied boot descend through soot. But soon the sand of the snow drifted into my eyes, and, though I stared toward the fireplace and around the flickering room where the black sack-like stocking hung, I was asleep before the chimney trembled and the room was red and white with Christmas. But in the morning, though no snow melted on the bedroom floor, the stocking bulged and brimmed; press it, it squeaked like a mouse-in-a-box; it smelt of tangerine; a furry arm lolled over, like the arm of a kangaroo out of its mother's belly; squeeze it hard in the middle, and something squelched; squeeze it again - squelch again... And a whistle to make the dogs bark to wake up the old man next door to make him beat on the wall with his stick to shake our picture off the wall. And a packet of cigarettes: you put one in your mouth and you stood at the corner of the street and you waited for hours, in vain, for an old lady to scold you for smoking a cigarette and then, with a smirk, you ate it. And, last of all, in the toe of the stocking, sixpence like a silver corn. And then downstairs for breakfast under the balloons!

DYLAN THOMAS (1914-1953)
FROM *"A PROSPECT OF THE SEA"*

SPECIAL GIFTS

One of the best parts of Christmas is
coming home to find lumpy carrier bags
on the doorstep.

MARION GARRETTY, b.1917

❄

He [Paddington] wasn't quite sure which he
had enjoyed most. The presents, the Christmas
dinner, the games, or the tea - with the special
marmalade-layer birthday cake Mrs Bird had
made for him. Pausing on the corner half-way
up, he decided he had enjoyed giving his own
presents best of all.

MICHAEL BOND
FROM *"MORE ABOUT PADDINGTON"*

❄

To receive a present handsomely and in a right
spirit, even when you have none to give in
return, is to give one in return.

LEIGH HUNT (1784-1859)

❄

24 December, 1954

Oh, how nice it would be, just for today and tomorrow, to be a little boy of five instead of an ageing playwright of fifty-five and look forward to all the high jinks with passionate excitement and be given a clockwork train with a full set of rails and a tunnel.

NOËL COWARD (1899-1973)
FROM *"DIARIES"*

❄

DREAM MAGIC

The magic of Christmas is a powerful magic indeed. . .

Christmas magic reunites scattered families, causes perfect strangers to greet one another. . . Now is the time when children reveal their impossible desires. Little girls are not afraid to ask for ponies; little boys dream of space ships that will really fly to the moon. Even sensible adults are caught up in the spirit of what-might-be. . .

So the sense of excitement grows until Christmas morning dawns at last, making clear what all the preparations and waiting meant. The miracle has happened after all: it is the birth of Christ, which took place nearly 2,000 years ago, but still happens in the hearts of men every Christmas of every year.

"The age of miracles past?" wrote Thomas Carlyle. "The age of miracles is forever here!"

Faith in miracles is the true magic of Christmas.

FROM *"THE MERRIMENT OF CHRISTMAS"*

Christmas day, 1918

This morning was typical Christmas weather, a
white frost and a brilliant sky. I have been to a
children's party at Dolly's where we played
games. It was happy and yet sad to an old man.
One remembers so many Christmas parties as
far back as fifty years and more ago and oh!
where are the children that played at them?
There is a tall oak clock ticking away at the end
of this room; the man who cleaned it the other
day said it was the oldest he had ever handled.
It has seen many more Christmasses than I
have, four or five times the number, and still it
ticks unconcernedly, marking the passage of the
hours and the years. Doubtless it sounded the
moment of my birth as it will do that of my
death. Remorselessly it ticks on, counting the
tale of the fleeting moments from Yule to Yule.
Yes, Christmas is a sad feast for the old, and yet
- thanks be to God who giveth us the victory -
one is full of hope.

SIR HENRY RIDER HAGGARD (1856-1925)
FROM *"DIARY 1914-1925"*

❄

A MOTHER'S GIFT

Soggy with self-pity, we went to bed on Christmas Eve without even having decorated a tree. On Christmas morning we awoke without expectation and rose with reluctance. Sullenly we fled our icy bedroom with our clothes in our arms, to dress behind the parlor heater. And look: In the corner of the parlor a tree hung with popcorn and cranberries and tinsel flickered with candles.

There were packages under it - small and few, but packages. We fell upon them. A sweater for each of us, a pair of home-knitted heavy wool socks, a jackknife for my brother, a deck of Flinch cards for me, a sockful each of crinkled Christmas candy and jelly beans.

Looking up from tearing open packages, I saw our mother standing in the doorway watching us. Her hands were fists in her apron pockets, and I read her look: she was afraid we would find the little she had been able to provide

meager and disappointing . . . she had been
working at that sparse Christmas ever since our
father went away. . . .

WALLACE STEGNER, b.1909
FROM *"THE CHRISTMAS TREASURY AND PERSONAL*
FAMILY RECORD"

FAMILY PARTY!

Who can be insensible to the outpourings of good feeling, and the honest interchange of affectionate attachment which abound at this season of the year. A Christmas family-party! We know nothing in nature more delightful! There seems a magic in the very name of Christmas. Petty jealousies and discords are forgotten; social feelings are awakened, in bosoms to which they have long been strangers; father and son, or brother and sister, who have met and passed with averted gaze, or a look of cold recognition for months before, proffer and return the cordial embrace, and bury their past animosities in their present happiness. Kindly hearts that have yearned towards each other but have been withheld by false notions of pride and self-dignity, are again reunited, and all is kindness and benevolence!

CHARLES DICKENS (1812-1870)
FROM *"SKETCHES BY BOZ"*

❄

Letters, telephone calls, trains and planes and cars and coaches - a net flung over the world at Christmas, bonding it with love.

HELEN EXLEY, b.1943

❄

The most remarkable aspect of Christmas is that no matter which country you are in, the hand of friendship reaches out to everyone. It is a time when whole families - sometimes ranging from great grandmother down to the youngest babe in arms - come together to celebrate. Most do it for religious reasons; others just for the pleasure of the season. Stand at an airport in the days preceding Christmas and watch the homecomings: the rapturous hugs for Mum and Dad and the joy on their children's faces at being home.

Christmas is the one time of all the year that can bring people together, a time when all can proclaim "Joy To The World".

LYNN BYRON AND JO SEAGAR
FROM *"THE CHRISTMAS BOOK"*

❄

Glorious time of great Too-Much.

LEIGH HUNT (1784-1859)

❄

Christmas is the one time when people are allowed to be plain *silly*.

PAM BROWN, b.1928

❄

Christmas itself may be called into question If carried so far it creates indigestion.

**RALPH BERGENGREN,
FROM** *"THE UNWISE CHRISTMAS"*

❄

We are having the same old things for Christmas dinner this year . . . relatives.

MARK TWAIN (1835-1910)

❄

Christmas is mothers saying, "Don't fight this is the season of good will."

LINDA DICKINSON, AGE 10

❄

YESTERDAY'S CHRISTMAS

As we sit in our dark and dusty chamber, made bright to-day by sprigs of holly and mistletoe (we shall increase Mrs. Scrubs our landress' Christmas-box for her thoughtfulness), we can almost fancy that our white hair is auburn once again, and that those rows of dusty books are the bright oak panels of our dear old country home. Our pinched-up fire expands into a capacious ingle, and that mixture of coke and slates becomes huge blocks of bituminous coal, and gnarled logs that sparkle and sputter as they are vanquished by the fire. The soot upon the dirty windowpanes crystallizes, and assumes a thousand shapes of beauty, as though the frost had breathed upon it, and changed it to the pure dew which rises from Camber Vale! The hum of London streets becomes a measured harmony, and we can hear one of our countryside carols as plainly as though it were sung by the small detachment of our village choir upon which we looked the last Christmas-

day we spent in the old home. Fourteen years
ago, and yet we can see that group as though
they stood before us in the body....

Only to think! little Lucy Lot is now the
buxom wife of George Weathers, the butcher,
and the proprietor of a brace of babies.

Where are the singers gone? Where the song?
Where the old home? Gone! But we have been
made happy thinking of the Christmas time.

M. L., 1855

❄

But our fun had not yet ended. At a signal from my mother we followed her into the dining-room. Here a sight awaited us that surprised us one and all. The room was brilliantly lighted up with wax candles on sconces from the walls; and on the table there was placed a great Christmas Tree, hung all over with little lamps and bon-bons, and toys and sweetmeats and bags of cakes. It was the first tree of the kind that I and my companions had ever seen. It was quite a new-fashion the Christmas Tree; and my brother Tom, who had just come home from Germany, had superintended its getting up and decoration. With what shouts of joy we hailed the pretty Christmas Tree, and with what glee and laughter we began to search among its twinkling lights and bright green leaves for the toys and sweetmeats that were hanging there, each one with a name written on its envelope, I can hardly tell you. But we were very merry, I know, and very grateful to our dear mother for her care in providing this delightful surprise as a finish to our merry evening's sports.

ANONYMOUS, FROM *"THE CHRISTMAS TREE"*, **1857**

❄

As well might we dance without music, or attempt to write a poem without rhythm, as to keep Christmas without a Christmas tree.

FROM THE *"WEEKLY PRESS"*, **1877**

❄

... after dinner the Uncles sat in front of the fire, loosened all buttons, put their large moist hands over their watch chains, groaned a little and slept. Mother, aunts and sisters scuttled to and fro, bearing tureens. Auntie Bessie, who had already been frightened, twice, by a clock-work mouse, whimpered at the sideboard and had some elderberry wine. The dog was sick. Auntie Dosie had to have three aspirins, but Auntie Hannah, who liked port, stood in the middle of the snowbound back yard, singing like a big-bosomed thrush. I would blow up balloons to see how big they would blow up to; and, when they burst, which they all did, the Uncles jumped and rumbled. In the rich and heavy afternoon, the Uncles breathing like dolphins and the snow descending, I would sit among festoons and Chinese lanterns and nibble dates and try to make a model man-o'-war, following the Instructions for Little Engineers, and produce what might be mistaken for a sea-going tramcar.

DYLAN THOMAS (1914-1953)
FROM *"A CHILD'S CHRISTMAS IN WALES"*

❄

There is a small and vulgar fashion of discouraging carols at Christmas. People who chat cheerfully amid all the infernal noises of the underground, people who endure the rattle of a thousand vehicles over a stony road, pretend that they dislike the sound of Christmas carols.

To pretend to like a thing may be a sin: to

pretend to dislike a thing comes near to
the sin against the Holy Ghost. At least it may
be hoped that a few at this season may
listen to these songs: they are the last echoes
of the cry that renewed the world.

G. K. CHESTERTON (1874-1936)
FROM *"THE SPIRIT OF CHRISTMAS"*

❋

...a really close examination of all the facets and
feelings of Christmas usually ends up by
breeding not contempt but its opposite, a slow
snowballing of approval and applause. In spite
of all our experience of commerce gone
tastelessly amok, of sore feet and emptied
pockets in a dictated and mainly senseless
shopping chore, and of over-eating and all that -
one may finally recognize what was not clear
before: that it would be dangerous to do
without Christmas, that a respite from winter
and a sense of occasion are vitally and
humanly necessary.

WILLIAM SANSOM
FROM *"CHRISTMAS"*

❋

Midnight strikes. You hear it in the silence of Christmas night as you hear it at no other time. The great day has come to an end.

If you are abroad you will be startled by your own solitude. You will understand how truly is Christmas the festival of the home. A man or a woman alone kindles a feeling of sympathy in your breast; you begin to think a tragedy of friendlessness around them.

You pass the cab-stand. It is empty. You pass the public-house. It is shut. The buses have ceased running. You quicken your steps, and hasten to your own home, which you have only quitted because you want to see what London looks like on Christmas night. As you pass the policeman you involuntarily say, "Merry Christmas to you." The policeman answers, "Same to you, sir," Perhaps you put your hand in your pocket. It is past midnight, and Boxing Day has dawned.

FROM *"THE VICTORIAN CHRISTMAS BOOK"*

❄

KEEPING CHRISTMAS

How will you your Christmas keep?
Feasting, fasting, or asleep?
....Be it kept with joy or pray'r,
Keep of either some to spare;
Whatsoever brings the day,
Do not keep but give away.

ELEANOR FARJEON (1881-1965)

Forget, forgive, for who may say that Christmas day may ever come to host or guest again. Touch hands!

WILLIAM H. H. MURRAY
FROM "*JOHN NORTON'S VAGABOND*"

❄

Are you willing to forget what you have done for other people, and to remember what other people have done for you; to ignore what the world owes you, and to think what you owe the world; to put your rights in the background, and your duties in the middle distance, and your chances to do a little more than your duty in the foreground; ... to own that probably the only good reason for your existence is not what you are going to get out of life, but what you are going to give to life; to close your book of complaints against the management of the universe, and look around you for a place where you can sow a few seeds of happiness - are you willing to do these things even for a day? Then you can keep Christmas.

HENRY VAN DYKE (1852-1933)
FROM "*SPIRIT OF CHRISTMAS*"

❄

THE WHOLE YEAR THROUGH

Would that Christmas lasted the whole year through (as it ought), and that the prejudices and passions which deform our better nature, were never called into action among those to whom they should ever be strangers!

CHARLES DICKENS (1812-1875)

❄

I sometimes think we expect too much of Christmas Day. We try to crowd into it the long arrears of kindliness and humanity of the whole year. As for me, I like to take my Christmas a little at a time, all through the year. And thus I drift along into the holidays - let them overtake me unexpectedly - waking up some fine morning and suddenly saying to myself: “Why, this is Christmas Day!”

DAVID GRAYSON

❄

Somehow not only for Christmas
But all the long year through,
The joy that you give to others
Is the joy that comes back to you.
And the more you spend in blessing
The poor and lonely and sad,
The more of your heart's possessing
Returns to make you glad.

JOHN GREENLEAF WHITTIER (1807-1892)

❊

I will honour Christmas in my heart, and try to keep it all the year.

CHARLES DICKENS (1812-1870)

❊

Ring out the old, ring in the new,
Ring, happy bells, across the snow:
The year is going, let him go;
Ring out the false, ring in the true.

Ring out the grief that saps the mind,
For those that here we see no more;
Ring out the feud of rich and poor,
Ring in redress to all mankind.

ALFRED, LORD TENNYSON (1809-1892)

❄

Christmas is special. Christmas is magic. It is a time of warmth and peace. A season when we can revel unashamedly in nostalgia and tradition. The cynics amongst us have described Christmas as a period of preparations, invitations, anticipations, relations, frustrations, prostration and recuperation! But to most of us it is, above all else, a time of celebration. It always has been, and let's hope it always will be.

GYLES BRANDRETH
FROM *"THE CHRISTMAS BOOK"*

❄